Newland Church

PARISH CHURCHES OF THE FOREST OF DEAN

Mike Salter

CONTENTS

Staunton Church

INTRODUCTION

The few people living in the Forest of Dean in Saxon times seem to have adopted Christianity by the 5th century. In late Saxon times the area came under the bishopric of Hereford, remaining so until Gloucester Abbey was made a cathedral in 1540. There were perhaps half a dozen churches around the fringe of the Forest plateau by the late 11th century, some or all of them perhaps built of wood. The only surviving feature in any of the churches which definitely predates the 1140s, however, is the cubical font at Staunton.

The early churches were all rebuilt in the second half of the 12th century and several more were established. These buildings were still sparsely distributed but what remains of them suggests they were above average in size, complexity of layout, and standard of fittings. Lancaut is the only unaltered example of the usual humble chapel with two dimly lighted chambers separated by an arch, the eastern part being the altar space or sanctuary, and the west part a nave for laymen to stand in, seating then being unknown. The small windows and other openings would be round headed and the floor would be of dirt which was recovered with rushes once a year with appropriate ceremony.

Before 1200 the naves at Hewelsfield, English Bicknor, Staunton, and St Briavels were enlarged by adding aisles and the latter three were once all cruciform with a central tower and transepts between the nave and chancel. Only the Staunton tower now survives but all four retain arcades with simple round arches. Longhope has a tower at the west end of the nave, the position which was to become the norm in the later medieval period, while Ruadean has a tympanum depicting St George and the dragon over the re-set south doorway.

Drybrook Church

Coleford: Tower of the old church.

In the 13th century a second aisle was added at St Briavels and Staunton and long new naves and chancels were built at Tidenham and Awre. The latter has an aisle with several lancet windows, for the pointed arch was now in vogue. Later in the century lancets were placed together in pairs as at Abenhall and then tracery evolved by piercing the spandrel between the heads of the lights. Eventually geometrical and floral patterns were developed in the window heads. The large churches with long chancels, wide aisles, and lofty west towers at Lydney and Newland, the detached tower at Westbury, and the SW corner tower at Mitcheldean are late 13th century. Work upon the spires continued well into the 14th century. The church itself at Westbury was rebuilt in c1300, and so were those at Little Dean and Longhope, transepts being added at the latter.

The Perpendicular architectural style with four-centered arches and simpler window tracery types with an emphasis on the vertical first appeared in the Forest of Dean with the new church built at Newnham in the 1360s, the splendid tower and spire at Ruadean, and the tower, north aisle, and north chapel of c1380-1420 at Little Dean. There are 15th century towers at Huntley and Blaisdon. More important is the work at Mitcheldean of c1460 where an outer north aisle was added, and the arcades and roofs renewed. Large windows of this period were inserted at several other churches.

Just two new churches were built in the Forest of Dean between 1300 and 1800, a 16th century chapel at Bream, and the 18th century church at Blakeney, neither of which have survived. The industrial revolution brought about an increase in population and the creation of new settlements. Many non-conformist chapels were established in the 18th century, and the 19th century saw the building of over a dozen new parish churches and the rebuilding of many of the older ones. Two of the earliest new churches were Coleford and Parkend which took an unusual octagonal form. Some of the others have very wide naves, as at Blakeney, Cinderford, and Soudley. Good examples of the High Victorian style with marble columns and much decoration are the churches of Flaxley, Clearwell, Huntley, and Newnham.

3

The Miner's Brass, Newland Church.

Brass of a knight in Newland Church.

Although bare to start with, the churches gradually filled up with furnishings, fittings, and monuments. From the 14th century onwards chancels were normally closed off by screens which often carried lofts called rood-lofts from the rood or crucifixion which was mounted upon them. The staircases in the walls giving access to the lofts often remain long after the lofts themselves have been dismantled. The lofts were used by the musicians who played upon woodwind, brass, and string instruments before organs became common in the 19th century. They were also used for performing religious plays, which were particularly important before sermons became the norm in the 16th century. Medieval pulpits are rare, but two have survived, that at Staunton being of stone and reached from a stair serving the roodloft and tower belfry. Several churches have a few late medieval benches, and several have some fragments of medieval stained glass. Glass of the 19th and 20th centuries, however, is much more common. Most churches had a chest like that at Awre used for keeping valuable plate and vestments. There are fonts surviving from almost every period. The most notable are the Late Norman ones at Newnham and Tidenham, the latter cast in lead. Features of the 17th and 18th centuries mostly are chandeliers, hatchments (boards with coats of arms), and galleries. The latter were often removed during Victorian restorations along with high box pews.

The effigy of a 13th century priest at Newland is the earliest monument now surviving. Newland also has several other tombs and a brass of great interest dating from the 15th or 16th century which depicts a Forest of Dean miner. There are three medieval effigies at English Bicknor, and other monuments at St Briavels and Lydney. No tomb chests of the period 1540-1700 remain, but from the 17th century onwards are many tablets, some of which are adorned with small figures, symbols of death, architectural surrounds, heraldry, etc. Several churchyards have a fine collection of headstones and tomb chests bearing a variety of motifs as well as inscriptions.

A GLOSSARY OF TERMS

Baroque	- A whimsical and odd form of the Classical style.
Beakhead	- Decorative motif of bird or beast heads.
Calvary	- Crucifixion scene, sometimes with three crosses.
Carolean	- The time of Charles I and Charles II (1626-85).
Chamfer	- A slope made by cutting off a right angled edge.
Chancel	- The eastern part of a church used by the clergy.
Chapel-of-ease	- Chapel administered from and by a parish church.
Clerestory	- The upper storey of a church, with windows.
Collar-Beam	- Tie-beam used higher up, nearer the roof apex.
Communion Rail	- A wooden rail around or in front of an altar.
Cruciform Church	- A cross-shaped church with transepts.
Dado	- Decorative covering of lower part of a screen.
Dressings	- The cut stones used for openings and corners.
Embrasure	- An opening through the thickness of a wall.
Flamboyant	- Late Medieval French architectural style.
Four-Centered-Arch	- Arch with curves drawn from four compass points.
Gothick	- Imitation late medieval style of c1740-1830.
Hoodmould	- Moulding over an arch to throw off rainwater.
King-Post	- Upright timber connecting tie- and collar-beams.
Lancet	- Long narrow single light window with pointed head.
Light	- A compartment of a window.
Nave	- The part of a church used by the congregation.
Norman	- English architectural style from 1066 to c1200.
Piscina	- Stone basin for rinsing out vessels after mass.
Plate Tracery	- Massive and elementary tracery of c1260-90.
Pre-Raphaelite	- Victorian imitation of late medieval style.
Rebate	- Rectangular notch cut in a jamb to take a door.
Reredos	- A structure behind an altar.
Respond	- A half-pier or half-column bonded into a wall.
Roll Moulding	- A moulding in the form of a continuous roll.
Tie-Beam	- Beam connecting roof slopes near their foot.
Tracery	- Intersecting ribwork in the head of a window.
Transept	- Projecting arm of a church containing an altar.
Tympanum	- Space between a doorway lintel and an arch above.
Victorian	- The time of Queen Victoria (1837-1901).
Wind Braces	- The struts strengthening the slopes of a roof.

Tomb of Jenkin Wyrall in Newland Church.

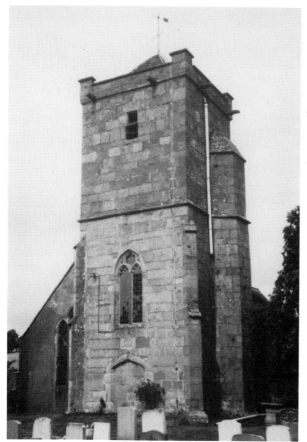

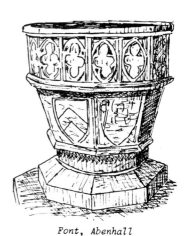

PLAN OF ABENHALL CHURCH

Font, Abenhall

Abenhall Church

GAZETTEER OF CHURCHES IN THE FOREST OF DEAN

ABENHALL *St Michael*   SO 671175

There is no real village at Abenhall, and the church, which is only
1.5km south of Mitcheldean, is accompanied by just two farmhouses.
Originally, as built in the 13th century as a chapel-of-ease, the
church comprised a modest single chamber with large twinned lancet
windows in the side walls, a triple lancet west window, and an east
window of three lights with intersecting tracery. A south aisle
with a three bay arcade was added in the early 14th century. This
was shortened in the 19th century when a new east wall was built
and half of the easternmost arch blocked. West of the aisle is a
15th century tower with diagonal buttresses, a stair turret on the
south side, and a shield of the free miners' arms on the west side.
The organ recess and porch are Victorian, whilst the round headed
south doorway looks like re-set Norman work from an older building.

The 15th century font has quatrefoils in lozenges, and shields
with emblems of the free miners and smiths, and the arms of Warwick,
Buckingham, and Serjeaunt. The 14th century chancel north window
contains contemporary glass fragments, including a figure thought
to be St Catherine. The Pyrke family are commemorated by an early
18th century Baroque tablet and a brass to Richard Pyrke, d1609.

Alvington Church

ALVINGTON *St Andrew*   SO 603008

The chancel north window and the nave SW corner are Norman. They are just sufficient to indicate the size and shape of the church of that period. The west tower added in c1300 has an embattled top stage of the 17th or 18th century. The early 14th century south aisle is comparatively wide and has a three bay arcade with foliage capitals on the octagonal piers. A squint looks into the chapel to the east. This chapel was rebuilt during the heavy restorations of 1858 and 1890 and other contributions of that period are the south porch, two north vestries, the chancel arch, most of the windows, the font, and the reredos. There are tablets to Sir Robert Woodrof, d1808, William Clarkson, d1803, George Watkins, d1832, and Anne Noel, d1851.

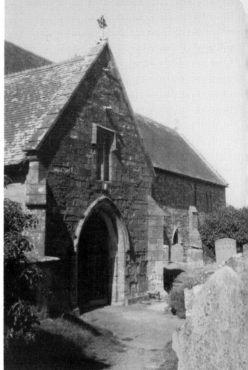

The Tower, Awre Church   *The Porch, Awre Church*

AWRE   *St Andrew*   SO 709081

The church lies among scattered farms in a loop of the Severn. It
has an embattled 15th century west tower with three stages divided
by string courses, diagonal buttresses, and a NE corner staircase
turret, and a slightly earlier south porch which appears to have
been intended to have had a priest's room above. A 13th century
doorway is re-set in the tower, and a window of the same period in
the porch, and indeed the long nave and chancel of equal width and
the north aisle are all of c1200-50. Of that period are the triple
lancet east windows of the aisle and chancel, the four north facing
single lancets, the tomb recess in the aisle, the six bay arcade
with round piers, the niche above the later medieval south doorway,
and the chancel arch with floriated capitals. The south windows and
buttresses of the nave are 15th century, as are the restored north
windows alternating with the older lancets. The screen dates from
c1500 and the rood stair may be an insertion of about that period.
The church was comparatively lightly restored by Waller and Son in
1875. Theirs is the chancel roof, and they restored the boarded
wagon roof of the nave and aisle. The octagonal font with trefoils,
quatrefoils and arcading is 15th century. There is a large ancient
chest carved out of a single trunk, supposedly once used for laying
out bodies recovered from the Severn. The reredos dates from 1892.
The monuments in the church include a slate tablet of 1670 and a
marble tablet by Henry Healey to Archdeacon Sandiford, d1826, and
outside is a good collection of typical Forest of Deam tomb stones.

8

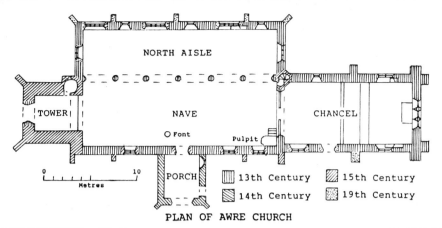

NORTH AISLE

TOWER

NAVE

CHANCEL

O Font

Pulpit

| | | | 13th Century | ▨ 15th Century |
| 14th Century | ▨ 19th Century |

PLAN OF AWRE CHURCH

AYLBURTON *St Mary*   SO 617019

A plaque on the chancel tells us "This chapel was removed from the place where it stood on the hill above nearly without alteration, 1856". So the plan may be basically the original, and the five bay south arcade, several of the windows, and the ogee-headed niche over the south doorway are all of c1290-1340, but the rockfaced outer walling is all typically Victorian. The priest's doorway, now mostly hidden behind a tank, may be older work of c1200. The font and stone pulpit are 15th century, and the aisle east window has fragments of medieval glass. There are Royal Arms of George III.

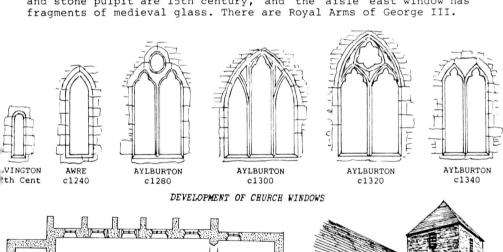

| .VINGTON th Cent | AWRE c1240 | AYLBURTON c1280 | AYLBURTON c1300 | AYLBURTON c1320 | AYLBURTON c1340 |

DEVELOPMENT OF CHURCH WINDOWS

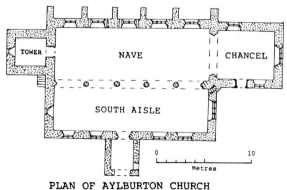

TOWER

NAVE

CHANCEL

SOUTH AISLE

PLAN OF AYLBURTON CHURCH

Aylburton Church

9

Beachley Church

BEACHLEY *St John*   ST 550913

This small cruciform church on an isthmus between the Severn and the
mouth of the Wye was built in 1833 to a design by Foster and Okeley.
It has lancet windows and a wooden rose window at the west end with
a tiny bellcote. Set inside are contemporary tablets by Tyley of
Bristol.

BERRY HILL *Christchurch*   SO 573129

This was the first 19th century church in the Forest of Dean, being
built in 1816. It has a nave and wide north aisle and a west tower
designed by Richard James with diagonal buttresses and Y-traceried
windows. The apsidal chancel with 14th century style windows was
added in 1885. Inside is a monument by Johnson to the Reverend
Procter, d1822.

BLAISDON *St Michael*   SO 704173

The medieval church was an aisle-less 13th century building with a
14th century east window and an embattled 15th century west tower
with diagonal buttresses and a short spire. Only the tower, plus
some early 16th century pews with a linenfold pattern on them, and
a chest dated 1709 with the name John Hayle, survived a rebuilding
of 1867-9 to a design by F.R. Kempson of Hereford. The cost, over
£2,000, was borne by Henry Crawshay. The church is built of Forest
stone with Bath stone dressings and comprises a nave, north aisle,
chancel, vestry, and south porch. The piers of the arcade have
flowers, leaves, animals, and birds carved on the capitals. There
are several 19th century tablets by Cook of Gloucester. The windows
contain stained glass of 1912 by Curtis, Ward, and Hughes, and of
1931 by Davies of Bromsgrove.

Blaisdon Church

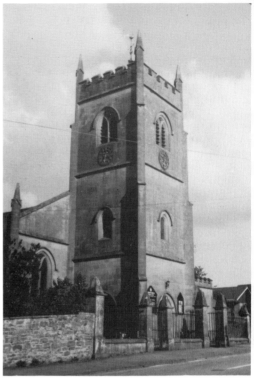

Berry Hill Church

BLAKENEY *All Saints*

SO 673072

This church was established in the early 18th century but in c1820 was rebuilt by Samuel Hewlett as a very wide structure with huge pointed windows and a tiny west tower. The apsidal altar space was added at the restoration of 1907. A weathered 15th century stoup serves as the font.

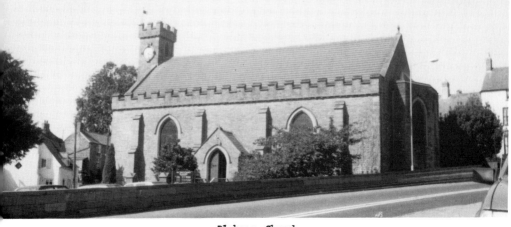

Blakeney Church

Bream Church

BREAM *St James*
SO 602055

The present church was built in 1860 to a design by William White. It comprises a chancel with plate tracery in the windows, a nave and north aisle having a four bay arcade with marble columns with big foliage capitals, and an unusually positioned SW corner bellcote. There are king-post and collar-beam roofs, and a vestry was added in 1891. The piscina in the chancel is a relic of the church that existed here in the 16th century. The font is somewhat later.

CINDERFORD *St John*
SO 653128

Cinderford only gained its own church in 1844 when St John's was built to a design by Edward Blore at the SW corner of the town. It is a rock-faced building with lancet windows lying in a very large graveyard. It comprises a wide nave and chancel with transepts and has a turret with an octagonal top surmounted by a spire between the nave and south transept. There is a cast iron west gallery and a fine 13th century style screen inside. The stained glass in the sanctuary is of 1938, and that in the south transept is of 1946, both being designed by ·D.B.Taunton of Hardman's. Two north windows have glass by Hugh B. Powell of 1966. The most notable monument is the tablet by Toleman of Bristol to Juliet Crawshay, d1848.

CINDERFORD *St Stephen*
SO 658138

The town's growth in the late 19th century prompted the building of a second church dedicated to St Stephen just south of the town centre in 1890-3. Designed by E.H.Lingen Barker, it has an aisled nave with four bay arcades and a clerestory, and is in a late 13th century style. The organ chamber and vestry were added in 1896.

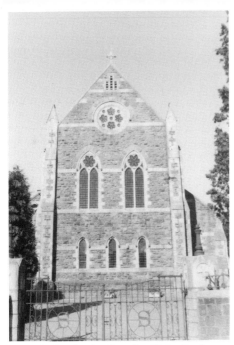

St Stephen's Church, Cinderford

St John's Church, Cinderford

CLEARWELL *St Peter* SO 572080

The present church, designed by John Middleton of Cheltenham, was built in 1866 for Caroline, Countess of Dunraven, the owner of the adjacent 18th century mansion called Clearwell Castle. The medieval church and the building which replaced it in 1829, designed by G.V. Maddox of Monmouth, lay on a different site. The church comprises an aisled nave with a tower standing at the west end of the south aisle, a chancel, and a south porch. The tower is surmounted by a spire 37m high. The outer walls are faced with local sandstone but the dressings are of white Bath stone. The interior has courses of blue and red sandstone alternating with white Bath stone, and there are Derbyshire, Italian and Irish marbles ,with Serpentine in the chancel. There is a great deal of fine sculpture such as the Alpha and Omega panels over the chancel arch, the reredos by Hardman, and the pulpit and font of Caen stone and sandstone. Some stained glass is by Hardman, but the south aisle east window is of 1959 by Edward Payne. There are encaustic tiles on the floor.

Clearwell Church

13

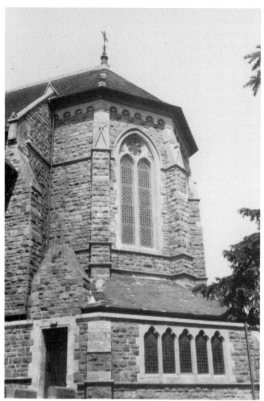

Coleford Church   *Drybrook Church*

COLEFORD *St John*   SO 575106

Coleford was a chapelry of Newland and only became an independent parish in 1876. In the middle of the town square is a tower which is the sole remnant of a church designed by Richard James built in 1821. It was an octagan similar to that at Parkend. The tower has diagonal buttresses, simple Gothick openings, and an embattled parapet with pinnacles. The church was restored in 1862 but was demolished two years after a larger new church on a more elevated site to the NW was built in 1880 by F.S.Waller. The latter has a big four bay nave, a two bay chancel, and north and south transepts with 13th century style windows. A lofty apsidal sanctuary was added in 1885 by S. Gambier-Parry. Notable features are the War memorial reredos of 1918 in carved oak by Sir Charles Nicholson, and the glass of 1958 by Francis Stephens in the east window.

DRYBROOK *Holy Trinity*   SO 648165

This church of 1817 has a wide nave, short chancel, an embattled west tower, and north and south porches. It lies on a shelf beside the Coleford to Cinderford road. There is intersecting tracery in the Gothick windows, and a west gallery inside with panelling upon classical columns. The east window glass is of 1922 by Bewsey. There are tablets to Elizabeth Harper, d1837, the Reverend Henry Nicholls, d1867, and the Reverend Henry Berkin, d1847.

14

English Bicknor Church   *Effigy of a priest, English Bicknor Church*

ENGLISH BICKNOR *St Mary*   SO 582158

The church lies in the outer bailey of a motte and bailey castle.
At a glance the church appears Victorian because the soft sandstone
outer walls are renewed except for the 13th century west tower with
an embattled 15th century upper part. So the interest of the church
lies in the interior. The four bay north arcade with plain rounded
arches with scallop capitals may go back to the 1140s, the probable
date of the castle earthworks, and it appears that the church was
then cruciform, and had, or was intended to have, a central tower.
The five bay south arcade is also Norman, but later, the scallop
capitals having leaves ending in volutes. Also Late Norman is the
particularly fine arch with chevrons at right angles to the wall and
beakheads, which lies at the east end of the north arcade. It must
surely be ex-situ, and may be a south doorway which was built with
the south arcade, being moved when the aisle was widened, although
it is unusually large and lacks a rebate. The chancel arch is 13th
century and the arch to the north chapel looks 18th century, having
a keystone. The south, or Machen, chapel has a screen of c1500 with
a boarded dado. Re-set in the north chapel is a pillar piscina of
c1200. Over the tower arch are the arms of George III. The stained
glass in the east window is of 1908 by Percy Bacon, and there is a
chandelier of c1900 imitating 18th century Dutch work. In the north
aisle are effigies of a priest wearing a chasuble and two women in
gowns. That with her feet resting on a dog is thought to be Cecilia
de Muchegros, c1300, and the other, with a heart, may be Harwisia
de Muchegros, c1350. There is a tablet of 1664 with cherubs in the
chancel, and a portrait bust medallion and weeping child by Symonds
to Edward Machen, d1778, in the Machen chapel.

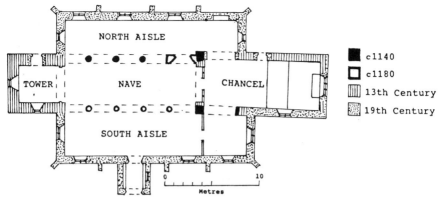

PLAN OF ENGLISH BICKNOR CHURCH

Legend:
- ■ c1140
- □ c1180
- ▥ 13th Century
- ▦ 19th Century

Scale: 0 — 10 Metres

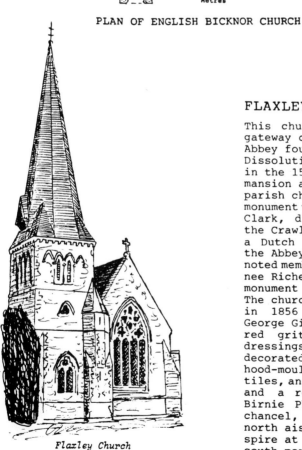

Flaxley Church

FLAXLEY *St Mary* SO 688154

This church originated as the gateway chapel of a Cistercian Abbey founded in c1150. At the Dissolution of the Monasteries in the 1530s the Abbey became a mansion and the chapel became a parish church. Within it are a monument with cherubs to Abraham Clark, d1683, and tablets to the Crawleys, and the Boeveys, a Dutch family who purchased the Abbey in 1648. Their most noted member, Catherine Boevey, nee Riches, d1720, also has a monument in Westminster Abbey. The church itself was rebuilt in 1856 to a design by Sir George Gilbert Scott. It is of red grit with Forest stone dressings and is very richly decorated inside with carved hood-mould stops, encaustic tiles, and a fine pulpit, font, and a reredos carved by J. Birnie Philip. It comprises a chancel, a three bay nave, a north aisle with a tower and spire at the west end, and a south porch.

Hewelsfield Church

HEWELSFIELD *St Mary Magdalene*   SO 568022

From the west the church appears to be nearly all roof because the
roof of the Norman nave continues down with unbroken slopes over
the narrow north aisle of c1200 and the small 13th century vestry
east of the 13th century south porch. The aisle has renewed lancet
windows and round piers carrying four round arches of two chamfered
orders. The inner south doorway is probably late 14th century, and
the west window is late 13th century. The central tower may be 12th
century in origin but has 13th century arches to east, west, and
north, the latter having a piscina in the east respond. The tower
top has been rebuilt. The north transept was enlarged to the north
in 1558, the original late 13th century north window then being
re-set. The extension is now walled off to form a vestry. The 13th
century chancel has an original priest's doorway and east window.
The south window is slightly later. Two nave south windows are 19th
century. The 13th century font has an octagonal scalloped bowl on
a round pedestal. There are tablets with heraldry to Edmund Bond,
d1742, and Anne Eddy, d1768.

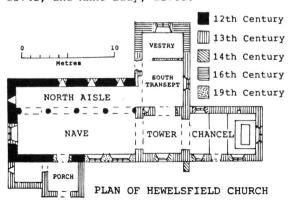

■ 12th Century
▨ 13th Century
▨ 14th Century
▤ 16th Century
▨ 19th Century

PLAN OF HEWELSFIELD CHURCH

Porch Entrance, Hewelsfield Church

17

HUNTLEY *St John The Baptist*

Only the 15th century west tower survived the rebuilding of what
was originally a Norman church in 1863. The work was largely paid
for by the rector Daniel Capper and designed by S.S.Teulon. A spire
was added to the tower. Interesting features of the exterior are
the Flamboyant tracery of the window in the shallow south transept
containing the organ, and the stair turret serving the vestry. There
is rich decoration within including alternate bands of red and white
stone, red mastic inlays, fine roofs, with gilded ribs and bosses
over the sanctuary, texts inscribed everywhere, and much carving by
Earp such as the deeply carved flowers on the arcade capitals and
the figures of the four evangelists on the arcade spandrels. The
lectern, pulpit, and reredos of alabaster and marble go well with
the church but are earlier. They were shown in the Great Exhibition
of 1851. There is stained glass by Lavers and Barraud. However the
nave and aisle windows with biblical scenes drawn in brown lines
with coloured shading and grisaille ornamentation were designed by
Teulon.

Huntley Church

Huntley Church

LANCAUT *St James*   ST 537965

The ruins of a tiny Norman church just 11.4m long internally lie on a shelf above the Wye in a rather delightful wooded spot 2.5km north of Chepstow. Although originally a chapel-of-ease it had attained full parochial status by the 13th century. The church is accessible easily enough on foot but there is no road to it, and as it lay some distance from any settlement it was finally abandoned in the 1860s. The chancel of c1180-1200 has been added to an earlier almost square nave. The east window opening has a roll-moulding around the inner side. The plain mullioned window, piscina, and priest's doorway in the chancel south wall are 14th century insertions. The stones of the nave doorway arch now lie on the ground within it. Two pointed openings of uncertain date in the west gable once contained bells. From this church has come the late 12th century lead font now set up in the Lady Chapel at Gloucester Cathedral. The bowl has an arcade in low relief with alternating figures and scrolls.

Lancaut Church

PLAN OF LANCAUT CHURCH

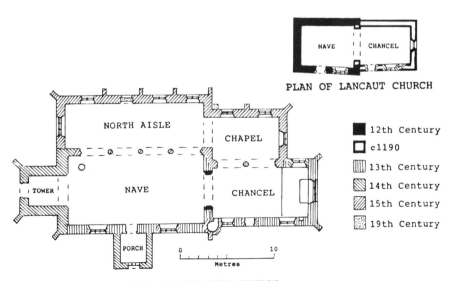

	12th Century
	c1190
	13th Century
	14th Century
	15th Century
	19th Century

PLAN OF LITTLE DEAN CHURCH

Little Dean Church

LITTLE DEAN *St Ethelbert* SO 673136

All that remains of the Norman church are the responds of the arch into the chancel. Otherwise the nave and chancel were rebuilt in c1300. The diagonally buttressed west tower and the north aisle with a four bay arcade were added at the end of the 14th century, and the Brayne chapel north of the chancel was added in c1411. It and the north aisle have two light square headed windows of the same type. The tower had a spire which was destroyed in a gale in 1894. There are original wagon roofs with ribs and bosses in the nave and chancel. At the SE corner of the nave is the rood stair. The outer entrance of the 14th century porch has been blocked and the room converted into a vestry. Upon it are mass sundials. The church has suffered only minimal 19th century restoration. There are fragments of medieval glass in some of the north windows. The font has an 18th century bowl on a 17th century base. In a case is a pair on tunicles of c1500 sewn together to make a pall or altar cloth. In the chapel is a 17th century table. In the chancel is a tablet by T.Rickets of Gloucester to Thomas Pyrke, d1752, and there is another Pyrke monument high up in the nave. There are several noteworthy tomb stones in the graveyard. One records a policeman killed whilst apprehending poachers and another recalls the death of four youths in a pit accident.

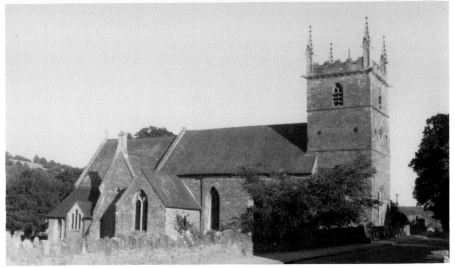

Longhope Church

LONGHOPE *All Saints*   SO 684198

Despite the fairly heavy restoration in the 1860s by A.W.Maberley
when the north vestries were added and the east window was provided
with glass by Clayton and Bell, the church has considerable medieval
interest. The lower parts of the four stage west tower are Late
Norman with mid-wall pilaster buttresses and one original southern
window. Remains of one window show the nave north wall is partly
Norman too, so the nave was always as wide as it is now. A recess
in the north transept east wall contains an effigy of a priest of
c1300 in eucharistic vestments. Perhaps it was he who rebuilt the
chancel as wide as the nave, added the transepts, and provided a
new tower arch. The porch and several windows, though, are early
14th century, and the tower top is probably late 14th century. The
chancel has an original priest's doorway and south lancet, plus a
15th century south window, but the chancel arch is Victorian. There
are Royal Arms of William III, early 19th century commandment boards,
and a painted tablet with a flat obelisk and urn to Josiah Bright,
d1777. In the churchyard is a mortar which served as the font from
the 1660s to the 1860s, when a new font was provided inside.

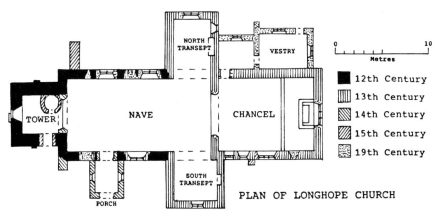

PLAN OF LONGHOPE CHURCH

	12th Century
	13th Century
	14th Century
	15th Century
	19th Century

*Lydbrook
Church*

LYDBROOK *Holy Jesus* SO 605517

The church nestles against a steep hillside. It was built in 1851 to a 14th century style design by Henry Woodyer, and has an aisled nave with a low clerestory, a west tower with a saddleback roof, a south porch, and a chancel. The roofs have a complex pattern of wind-braces and there are scissor-beam trusses in the chancel. The window tracery is mostly in the Geometrical style. The church was restored in 1904 by M.H.Medland, and an organ chamber was added in 1913 by A.H. Pearson.

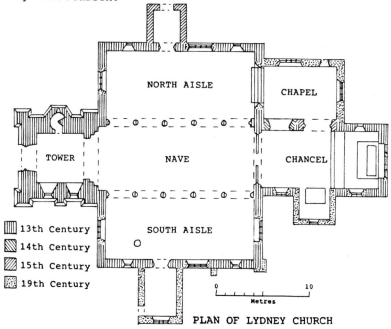

NORTH AISLE

CHAPEL

TOWER

NAVE

CHANCEL

SOUTH AISLE

||||| 13th Century
\\\\ 14th Century
//// 15th Century
▒▒ 19th Century

0   10
Metres

PLAN OF LYDNEY CHURCH

22

The west tower, aisled nave with five bay arcades, and the chancel are all 13th century. They form a building of considerable size, mainly owing to the great width of the aisles, perhaps a result of patronage by the Beauchamp and Talbot families who held manors in Lydney. However, the exterior is very restored and is not of much interest or beauty except for the splendid tower. The west doorway with orders of sunk quadrant mouldings suggests the tower, which has clasping corner buttresses, and a polygonal stair turret on the north side, was begun c1280. The spire may not have been completed until c1350. It was restored in the 1850s. The north chapel was probably added to serve a chantry of the Holy Cross endowed in 1375 by John and Julia Chardborough, and the north porch may have been added in about the same period. The chapel was rebuilt in the 1850s to serve as a choir vestry and organ space, but was restored as a chapel in 1940. At the time of the Victorian restoration the church was said to have been packed with high pews, although a contemporary painting shows it almost devoid of woodwork except a high pulpit. There are fine old wagon roofs over the nave and aisles. Over the north chapel arch are the arms of the Wynter family. The font is 15th century. There are Royal Arms of William III and Mary II, and a hatchment and a banner of Lord Bledisloe. Several windows have glass by Hardman, whilst the east windows have glass of 1946 by Smith, including the scene of the Franz Josef Glacier in New Zealand. Another window of 1938 is by Joseph Bell. Although inscribed with the year 1630 the female effigy holding a heart is 14th century. Poole Bathurst, d1792, is commemorated by a mourning female by T.King of Bath, and there is a tablet by Paty of Bristol to Mrs Bragg, d1793. Outside is a fine collection of interesting churchyard tombstones.

*Lydney
Church*

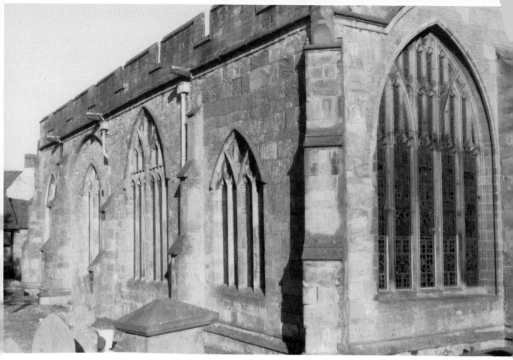

The North Aisle, Mitcheldean Church

MITCHELDEAN *St Michael*   SO 664186

Of the original 12th or 13th century nave only the west wall still remains. The tower at the SW corner, and the porch south of it are late 13th century, and there must have been a south aisle by that period, although the present aisle is early 14th century. Then a north aisle was added, along with the top two stages of the tower and the very lofty spire. In c1460 the church was remodelled. New arcades were provided, and an outer north aisle added. There are particularly fine roofs of this period with ribs, plastered panels, bosses, and angels holding shields. On the south side a stair turret was added to give access to the loft upon a screen which ran right across the whole width of the building. The stair continues down to give access to a vaulted bone-hole below the south aisle. The screen is alas gone, and the present short screen is 19th century, as are the chancel it closes off and the vestry to the north. A 15th century painting of the Last Judgement with scenes of the life of Christ set on wooden panels fills the space between the screen and the roof. The spire was rebuilt in 1760 by Nathaniel Wilkinson.

The huge west windows of the nave and outer north aisle contain early 20th century glass, but there are fragments of medieval glass in the north windows, and the south aisle has one window by Kempe. The east window has glass of 1968 by John Hayward. In front of the latter is a huge reredos erected in 1911 with life sized figures by W.G. Storr-Barber. The font is a copy of the original Norman font. The 15th century wooden pulpit is not now used and the seat from it is fixed to a wall. On the nave south wall are brasses of two wives of Thomas Baynham, Margaret, in a butterfly headdress, d1477, and Alice, d1518, in a dog-kennel headdress. There is a Baroque tablet in the south aisle to Elizabeth Holmes, d1758, and in the chancel is an 18th century tablet by Bryan of Gloucester.

The huge west windows of the nave and outer north aisle contain early 20th century glass, but there are some fragments of medieval glass set in the north windows, and one window in the south aisle has glass by Kempe, whilst the main east window glass is of 1968 by John Hayward. In front of the latter is a huge reredos erected in 1911 with life sized figures by W.G.Storr-Barber. The font is a copy of a Norman font. The 15th century wooden pulpit is not now used and the seat from it is fixed to a wall. On the nave south wall are brasses of two wives of Thomas Baynham. Margaret, with a butterfly head-dress, died in c1477, and her successor Alice, d1518 is depicted wearing a dog-kennel head-dress. There is a Baroque tablet in the south aisle to Elizabeth Holmes, d1758, and in the chancel is an early 18th century tablet by the Gloucester craftsman Bryan.

Brasses in Mitcheldean Church

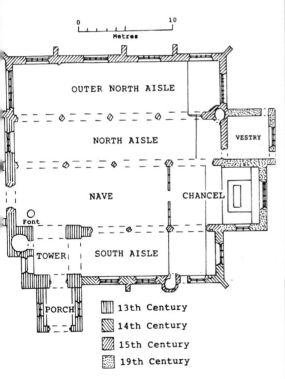

PLAN OF MITCHELDEAN CHURCH

OUTER NORTH AISLE

NORTH AISLE

VESTRY

NAVE

CHANCEL

Font

TOWER

SOUTH AISLE

PORCH

0   10
Metres

▥ 13th Century
▧ 14th Century
▨ 15th Century
▦ 19th Century

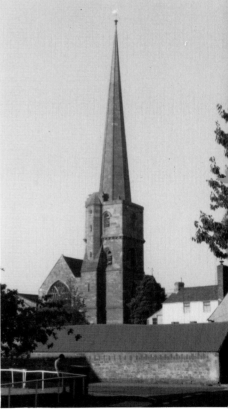

Mitcheldean Church from the South-West

Newland Church

NEWLAND *All Saints*   SO 553096

This church is thought to have been first established in the time
of rector Robert de Wakering (1215-37). A subsequent rector, Walter
Giffard, went on to become Archbishop of York. Most of the present
building, however, dates from c1280-1300 when Edward I's historian
John of London, a Westminster monk, was rector. It is the largest
church in the Forest of Dean and is nicknamed 'the Cathedral of the
Forest'. It comprises a west tower, a nave with five bay arcades
opening into very wide aisles, a south porch, chancel, and a south
chapel formed from an extension of the south aisle. Edward I added
the small chapel east of the porch to serve the chantry of King
Edward's service founded in 1305, and the north chapel was added
to serve the chantry of Our Lady's service founded by John Chinn,
d1416. In 1410 vicar William Smyth was struck down with a stroke,
and was unable to perform his duties so a coadjuter was appointed.
He must have been ineffective as the benefice was seized by William
Smyth and was only recovered with difficulty, whilst in 1426 the
Bishop of Hereford struck out at the practice of trading in the
spacious churchyard. This now forms a close surrounded by 17th and
18th century houses. The church was on the verge of ruin by 1861
when restored by William White. He provided a new east window with
glass by Clayton and Bell, a new clerestory, and various buttresses.
The south chapel east window and tower east window are unrestored
work of c1300 and the north chapel has an original east window too.
The tower has clasping buttresses which support diagonal buttresses
above. The top storey and the four spired corner pinnacles with
blank panelling, plus the plainer spired stair turret, are later
work, probably of c1360-80.

The fittings of interest include a locally made font of 1661
with shields on the bowl and leaves on the shaft, a fine chandelier
of c1725 probably made in London, some medieval tiles bearing the
de Bohun swan in the south chapel, hatchments of Thomas Wyndham,
d1752, and Charles Wyndham, d1801, some fragments of medieval glass,
a window of 1898 by Kempe in the chantry chapel by the porch, and
a Carolean communion rail.

The church has a particularly notable set of monuments. Effigies of Sir John Joce, c1344, and his wife, d1362, lie on a tomb chest in the south aisle. The knight wears armour similar to that of the Black Prince at Canterbury and his head rests on a helm with a head of a Saracen as a crest. The canopied panels on the sides of the tomb are renewed. Under the nave arcades are effigies of Robert de Wakering, and of an unknown priest of c1365. The effigy of Jenkin Wyrall, Forester of Fee, d1457, was brought into the church from the graveyard in 1950. An early 17th century forester with a bow, horn, dagger, and wide brimmed hat is depicted on an incised slab, also in the south aisle. In the south chapel is a very interesting brass. The female figure has an early 16th century style head-dress whilst the male figure has armour and short cropped hair typical of the 1440s, but a luxuriant beard, which was quite out of fashion in that period. It would appear that his figure was originally to Robert Gryndour and was later appropriated for Sir Christopher Baynham, knt, the name which is incised between the figures. It was probably then that the so called 'Miner's Brass' was added showing a helmet with mantling and a crest which represents a miner with a hod, pick, and a candle in a holder held in the mouth. Also within the chapel is a classical tablet to John Coster, d1719. The south chantry chapel contains a bust by T.Ricketts of Sir Edmund Probyn, Lord Chief Baron of the Exchequer, d1742, and other tablets to his family. The north chapel contains a Baroque monument to Benedict Hall of Highmeadow, d1688, and his wife Anne Wynter of Lydney, with the arms of the two families, while under the tower is a Baroque tablet to Christopher Bond, d1688, with laughing cherubs carrying cornucopia.

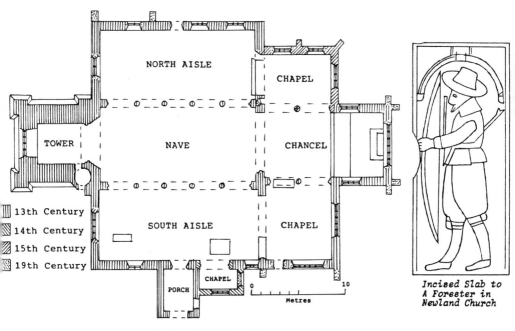

13th Century
14th Century
15th Century
19th Century

TOWER

NORTH AISLE

CHAPEL

NAVE

CHANCEL

SOUTH AISLE

CHAPEL

CHAPEL

PORCH

0   Metres   10

PLAN OF NEWLAND CHURCH

Incised Slab to A Forester in Newland Church

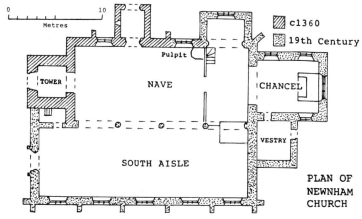

PLAN OF
NEWNHAM
CHURCH

NEWNHAM *St Peter*   SO 691115

Newnham was one of the five ancient boroughs of Gloucestershire.
It lay within Westbury parish and had a chapel-of-ease on the Nab
beside the Severn by 1018. The church only attained full parochial
status in the 14th century, by which time it was in danger of being
undermined by the river. In 1366 a new church was dedicated, having
been built on a fresh site further west donated by Humphrey de Bohun,
Earl of Hereford beside his castle or manor house. This church had
a nave, south aisle, chancel, north porch, and a west tower. It and
the castle were captured from the Royalists by Colonel Massey in
1644. During the commotion the Royalists exploded a powder keg in
the church, causing some damage, and driving all the combatants out.
The tower was given new battlements in the early 19th century, but
a new top stage and spirelet were added in 1874, when at a cost of
over £4,000 the church was mostly rebuilt except the tower and the
north side of the nave. The aisle was almost doubled in width and
a shallow north transept and a south vestry were added. The same
architect, Waller, restored the church again in 1881 after a fire
in which little but the remaining medieval parts survived intact.
Of the latter restoration are the reredos and pulpit and the four
bay arcade of polished granite piers with foliage capitals. Three
14th century windows containing 19th century glass are re-set in
the chancel, which has a painted boarded ceiling with bosses and
ribs. Relics of a 12th century church on the original site are the
font with an arcade of twelve niches containing the figures of the
Apostles, and a fragment of a doorway tympanum carved with The Tree
Of Life. A chancel arch of the same period or just a little later
also survived until 1874. There is a brass by Hardman in memory of
John Hill, d1894, and a mosaic and alabaster St George of 1919.

*Newnham
Church*

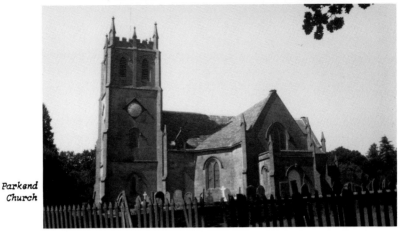

Parkend
Church

PARKEND *St Paul*   SO 620077

The church lies alone in a forest clearing some way SE of the town.
It was built in 1822 to an unusual but both practical and attractive
design by Richard James. It essentially forms an octagon about 15m
across with cruciform arms formed by a projecting sanctuary, west
end, and transepts. Beyond the sanctuary is a vestry, beyond the
transepts are small porches, and beyond the west end is an embattled
tower with diagonal buttresses rising to pinnacles. The windows are
Late Georgian Gothick and the central space has crossing ridge beams
and diagonal ribs meeting in a central boss like a rose. The west
end contains a gallery. The reredos has a painting of Christ mocked.
The altar rails were added at the restoration and redecoration of
1958 by R.W.Paterson. There are Royal Arms of George IV. By Cade
of Bristol are the monuments to the Reverend Henry Poole, c1857, and
John Langham, killed in the Crimean campaign in 1855.

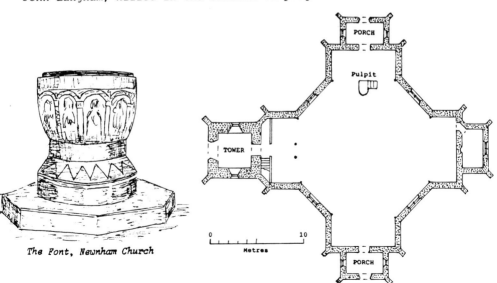

The Font, Newnham Church

PLAN OF PARKEND CHURCH

29

Redbrook Church

Tympanum at Ruadean Church

PRIMROSE HILL *Holy Trinity* SO 636044

This is a small brick building of 1903 with Romanesque windows and is hidden away in an estate north of Lydney. It is not of interest.

REDBROOK *St Saviour* SO 537099

This modest church in the style of c1300 lying beside the River Wye was built in 1873 to a design by J.P.Seddon. It has a wide chancel and nave, small transepts, a south porch, and a spired turret set betwen the nave and south transept. Notable features are the sanctuary floor tiles, the choir stalls with carved finials, and the stained glass of 1902 by W.Tower in the east window.

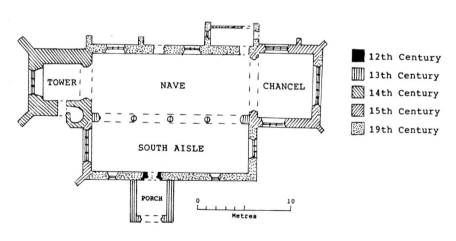

PLAN OF RUADEAN CHURCH

Ruadean Church

RUADEAN *St John The Baptist* SO 621177

The church lies on the edge of the forest plateau, commanding an extensive view to the west and north. The building was founded in c1110 but the earliest relic is the re-set south doorway of c1140. This has a splendid tympanum showing St George on horseback slaying the dragon. It was carved by the Herefordshire School of sculpture who also worked at Kilpeck, Brinsop, Leominster, and Stretton Sugwas. A small carved stone with two fishes discovered in a nearby house in the 1950s was probably also a relic of the church of this era.

The church was given a south aisle with a four bay arcade and a south porch in the 13th century and the piscina in the chancel is also of that period. The chancel and aisle west wall appear to have been rebuilt in the 15th century and much of the rest of the exterior of the church was renewed in 1890 by Waller and Son. However, the west tower with diagonal buttresses connected by flying buttresses to the spire are original late 14th century work. The plain font is of 1657, and the pulpit is also 17th century. A medieval tomb lies in a recess in the north wall. Tablets in the nave and chancel commemorate Richard Jelfe, d1769, Alice Smith, d1776, John Hankinson, d1637, Charles Bennett, d1829, and Hannah Davis, d1860. The fine set of churchyard monuments have been moved to facilitate grass cutting. A few remain propped against the wall.

St Briavels Church

Coffin lid at
St Briavels

ST BRIAVELS *St Mary*

SO 558047

The narrow south aisle with a five bay arcade of round arches on low round piers with scallop capitals, small clerestory windows set above the spandrels, and a lean-to roof, is Norman. Also Norman but of c1180-1200, are the four elaborately moulded arches of the original crossing tower, later taken down because it was unsafe and replaced by a porch-tower of c1830 on the south side designed by John Briggs. The north transept masonry may also be of c1200 but the end window is of c1300, when the south transept was rebuilt with an identical window. The 13th century also saw the addition of a narrow lean-to north aisle with a four bay arcade, and a new chancel. However, the restoration of 1861 by J.W.Hugall left only a piscina on the north side of the latter while the aisle gained new buttresses and windows. The vestry is also Victorian. Opening from the south aisle are 14th century stairs to the former loft of the now-removed screen.

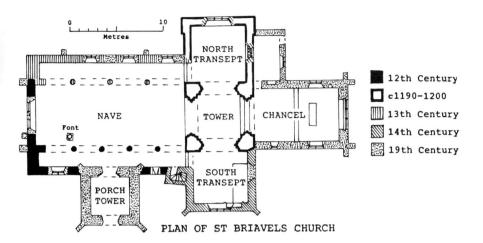

PLAN OF ST BRIAVELS CHURCH

Legend:
- ■ 12th Century
- □ c1190-1200
- ▤ 13th Century
- ▨ 14th Century
- ▦ 19th Century

The Norman font lies on an unusual sixteen lobed shelf. There are Royal Arms of Elizabeth II, an organ of 1922 by Nicholson of Worcester, and the east window glass is of 1899 by Powell. The tomb recess in the south transept contains a slab of c1300 carved with a cross, foliage, and a head. There are also remains of a late 16th century tomb with semi-reclining effigies of William Warren and his family, plus a tablet by Woolcott to Charles Court, d1819.

SOUDLEY *St Michael*   SO 060106

This rock-faced church of 1910 comprises simply a wide nave with a sanctuary at one end and a porch at the other. The side windows are paired lanced. The east window has glass of 1937 by Wilkinson.

Soudley Church

Staunton Church

STAUNTON *All Saints*   SO 552126

A relic of an 11th century church here is a crude font forming a
rough cube with a band of pellet mouldings. The central tower is
late 12th century and has original belfry openings and a corbel
table. Also 12th century is the north arcade, the three western
arches of which are blocked. Of the five arches, the eastern three
are pointed and must be later than the round arches to the west.
The tower arches were renewed in the early 13th century when the
chancel was rebuilt and a south aisle with a five bay arcade was
added. The transepts are 13th century in their present form, whilst
the tower upper stage, battlements, and pinnacles are 15th century.
The south aisle was widened in the 14th century so that the outer
wall is now flush with the transept end wall, and a south porch
was then added. The chancel has a blocked original arch in the south
wall which may have led to a chapel. Two others in the east wall
perhaps led to a vestry. The north transept or Lady Chapel has two
13th century image brackets and a trefoil headed piscina. The stone
pulpit of c1500 is an unusual feature, especially as it is reached
from the stairs serving the tower and the former loft over a screen.
The main east window has stained glass of 1862. The north transept
east window is by Kempe. Medieval glass survives in a tiny upper
window in the chancel east wall. In the chancel is a 13th century
tombstone with an incised cross and chalice. It was re-used later.

34

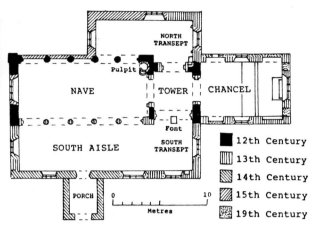

Pulpit, *Staunton Church*

PLAN OF STAUNTON CHURCH

Legend:
- ■ 12th Century
- ▥ 13th Century
- ▧ 14th Century
- ▨ 15th Century
- ▦ 19th Century

STOWE *St Margaret*   SO 563063

The north wall of a small medieval chapel is incorporated into the farmbuildings of Stowe Grange, north of St Briavels. The east wall stands ruinously to about 2.0m high and shows no sign of a window, whilst parts of the west and south walls stand about 1m high.

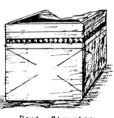

Font, *Staunton*

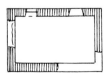

AN OF STOWE CHAPEL

Remains of Stowe Chapel

35

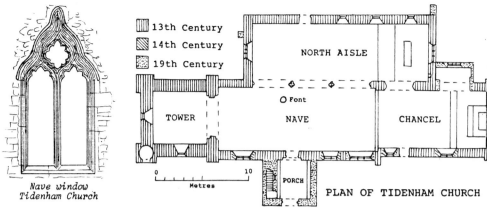

13th Century
14th Century
19th Century

NORTH AISLE

○ Font

TOWER

NAVE

CHANCEL

0 ____ 10
Metres

PORCH

PLAN OF TIDENHAM CHURCH

Nave window
Tidenham Church

Tidenham Church

TIDENHAM *St Mary*   ST 556958

Although it is mentioned in Domesday Book, the oldest part of the church is the early 13th century west tower with lancet windows and clasping buttresses. The equally plain upper part of the tower was added in the 15th century. It served as a beacon for navigation in the Severn estuary far below. Also 13th century are the nave and chancel, with a fine shafted south doorway and clasping buttresses at the east end. The wide north aisle with three arches on quatrefoil shaped piers without any capitals opening towards the nave, and one more arch opening into the chancel, is an addition of c1290-1310, whilst the ogee-headed south windows are of c1340. The church was heavily restored in 1858 by John Norton.

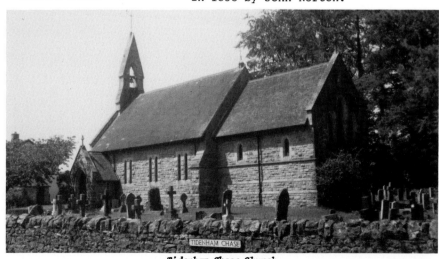

Tidenham Chase Church

36

Tutshill Church

Tidenham church contains a lead font which was cast from the same mould as that which once lay in Lancaut church not far away (see page 19). One south window contains pieces of medieval glass, and there is much more recent glass by Geoffrey Webb in the east window. There are numerous 19th century tablets, including those to Sarah Lowder, d1802, Selwyn Jones, d1805, Anna Camplin, d1812, Frances Morgan, d1831, and Drummond Thatcher, d1835.

TIDENHAM CHASE *St Michael*   SO 556988

This church lies almost alone in a clearing beside the B4228 3km north of the medieval church of Tidenham. It comprises a rock-faced nave, chancel, south porch, and bellcote, with lancets in ones, twos and threes, and was built in 1888 to a design by S. Gambier-Parry. Inside is a reredos with mosaics, and there is contemporary glass in the east window in the Pre-Raphaelite style.

TUTSHILL *St Luke*   ST 540095

Tutshill lies by the mouth of the Wye opposite Chepstow. It became fashionable in the early 19th century and in 1853 gained its own church designed by Henry Woodyer. The building comprises a nave and north aisle separated by an arcade copied from that at nearby Tidenham, a chancel with a two bay arcade to a north vestry and an organ chamber, a south porch, and a bellcote raised on a massive buttress on the south side of the chancel arch, with a staircase to the pulpit adjoining. The contemporary glass in the east window is probably by O'Connor. The north aisle window glass is of c1894.

Viney Hill Church

VINEY HILL *All Saints*   SO 655066

This church of local sandstone with an apsidal sanctuary was built
in 1867 to a design by Ewan Christian. It has a south aisle with
a roof continuous with that over the nave, but with a break of
slope, and a south porch and a non-projecting transept.

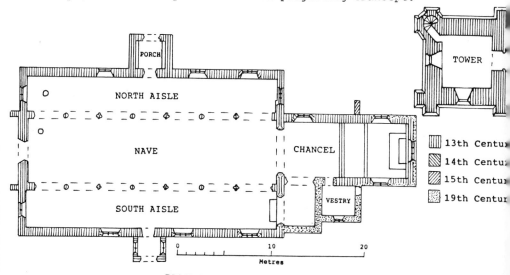

PLAN OF WESTBURY CHURCH

The Tower, Westbury Church   *West Front, Westbury Church*

WESTBURY *St Peter, St Paul, & St Mary*   SO 717139

Although much restored in 1862 and 1878, when the southern vestries were added, the church is almost all of c1300. It comprises a long aisled nave with a north porch and a chancel. The six bay arcades have alternating octagonal and quatrefoil shaped piers. The chancel has a rose-piscina but no other ancient features. The west wall contains a canopied niche containing a Calvary and a later medieval window. An inscription in a south aisle window "This church, built in A.D. 1530, was dedicated to the Virgin Mary", refers only to minor remodelling and the addition of a porch with a Tudor outer arch on this side. There is a 19th century font and another dated 1583 with the arms of Elizabeth I. Some of the pew bench ends have linenfold panels typical of c1520. There are two chandeliers of c1730, probably from Bristol. The chancel windows have glass of the 1860s, and a north aisle window has glass of 1906. There are many tablets to the Wintles, Boughtons, and Colchesters in the chancel.

Some 15m north of the north porch is the detached bell-tower, a massively built and heavily buttressed structure almost 9m square externally. It was built in c1270 and was perhaps intended as a military strong point. It was certainly used as such in 1644, when Colonel Massey captured it and a nearby fortified house from the Royalists. Upon the tower is a 14th century wooden framed spire.45m high which has been rebuilt several times and was last recovered with wooden shingles held with copper nails in 1937. The arch and roof marks on the east face are relics of the 14th century chantry chapel of St Mary, later used as a school and dismantled in 1862.

39

Westbury-on-Severn was an unusually large parish and required several chapels-of-ease, one of which, Newnham, later attained full parochial status. No medieval chapels have survived otherwise and in 1840 it was reported that three chapels and attendant clergy were urgently needed. A brick mission chapel dedicated to St Luke was eventually built at Chaxhill, and in 1908 and 1916 others were constructed at Rodley and Northwood.

WOOLASTON *St Andrew*   ST 587994

The church is first mentioned in 1131, and the long nave may have some Norman masonry, although the restored windows are of c1300. By the end of the 13th century the church had become cruciform with a tower on the north side of the nave, and a chapel on the south. The tower was rebuilt in the early 19th century and embattled in 1840. Between it and the heavily restored chancel is a vestry added in 1903. The chapel was absorbed into a south aisle built in 1829 by John Briggs, but became a chapel again in 1954. The arcade has polished granite columns with foliage capitals. The aisle now has transverse gables. The large porch west of it was rebuilt in 1859. The nave roof, the font, and the former priest's doorway now set up as a gateway facing the vicarage are all 14th century. There is a mutilated medieval panel depicting the Crucifixion. The pulpit of c1750 was brought over from Claycoton in Northamptonshire in 1966, and the screen of c1860 has come from the Church of the Venerable Bede at Sunderland. There are 19th century monuments to several members of the Hammond and Woodroffe families, and a tablet in a neo-Greek style to John Powles, d1844.

Nothing now remains of a chapel with a vaulted undercroft at Woolaston Grange, 1km south of the parish church.

Woolaston Church